This journal belongs to

Dates begun/completed

Living the Word

COMPANION JOURNAL

Edited by Sarah Christmyer

Ave Maria Press AVE Notre Dame, Indiana

Quotations on pages 23, 45, 67, 89, 111, 133, 155, 177, 199, 221, and 226 are taken from *Living the Word Catholic Women's Bible*, copyright © 2022 Ave Maria Press, Inc.

Scripture quotations are from the *Revised Standard Version of the Bible—Second Catholic Edition (Ignatius Edition)*, copyright © 2006 National Council of the Churches of Christ in the United States of America. Used by permission. All rights reserved.

_____

© 2023 by Ave Maria Press, Inc.

All rights reserved. No part of this book may be used or reproduced in any manner whatsoever, except in the case of reprints in the context of reviews, without written permission from Ave Maria Press®, Inc., P.O. Box 428, Notre Dame, IN 46556, 1-800-282-1865.

Founded in 1865, Ave Maria Press is a ministry of the United States Province of Holy Cross.

www.avemariapress.com

Hardcover: ISBN-13 978-1-64680-126-8

Cover and text design by Brianna Dombo.

Printed and bound in China.

Introduction	vii
Reading Log	xiii
Journal Pages: 100 Days in the Word	1
My Prayer Intentions	223
Women of the Word Index	227

The Word OF GOD BECAME INCARNATE. *We are called* TO PREACH THAT WORD DAY BY DAY BY DAY.

Servant of God Thea Bowman

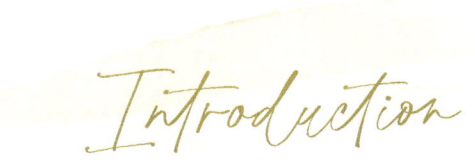

Introduction

Welcome to the *Living the Word Companion Journal*, which is designed to enhance your reading of the *Living the Word Catholic Women's Bible*, published by Ave Maria Press. That Bible offers more than two hundred pages of special features written for women, by women from many backgrounds. As you read, you will find yourself drawn again and again into a "company of women" who want to share with you what they have discovered through their own encounters with God's Word. If you don't already have a copy, you will certainly want to get one!

Journaling as you read scripture is a time-tested aid to taking God's Word to heart and growing in intimacy with him. The simple act of writing can help us remember and clarify what we read, form questions, apply it to our lives, and respond to God in prayer. Keeping a journal can foster gratitude and store up reasons for hope while building a record of God's work in our lives.

> WE HAVE BEEN GIVEN *Sacred Scripture* SO THAT GOD AND MAN MAY TALK TOGETHER; FOR WE SPEAK TO HIM WHEN WE PRAY; WE HEAR HIM WHEN WE READ THE DIVINE SAYING.
>
> St. Ambrose

FEATURES OF THE LIVING THE WORD COMPANION JOURNAL

This journal will help you grow closer to Jesus in his Word as you develop a regular habit of reading and praying with scripture:

- A simple, two-page format guides your journaling for 100 days of scripture reading, with room for observations and questions, applications and prayers.
- "Today's Living Word" is a daily scripture to inspire, encourage, and challenge you.
- Specially designed frames invite you to copy down or illustrate meaningful verses to remember from each reading.
- "Taking Stock" pages allow you to articulate the highlights of what you've learned in the past ten days—and be inspired by motivating quotes from the *Living the Word Catholic Women's Bible*.
- Prayer intentions and reasons for thanksgiving can be kept handy on pages 223–25.
- Once completed, the Reading Log at the front of this journal forms a "table of contents" to help you find what you have already written about particular passages.

GETTING STARTED

These tips will help you cultivate a habit of regular Bible reading. Some have been gleaned from a feature in the *Living the Word Catholic Women's Bible* called "Where Do I Start? A Beginner's Guide to Reading the Bible" (pages 1923–24).

1. *Prepare a space.* Pick a place you can reasonably set aside for a daily encounter with the Lord. Schedule a convenient time, and designate a shelf or basket to hold your Bible, this journal, a pen, and maybe a rosary and a favorite icon: anything you might need as you spend time with God.
2. *Set achievable reading goals.* Plan ahead for a week or a month so you'll always know what to read when you begin (see the suggestions in "Where Do I Start?" and the reading plans at the back of the *Living the Word Catholic Women's Bible*). If you choose to read a book of the Bible, read the introduction first and take note of any topical essays that might be found within it. See the Women of the Word Index in this journal or at the back of the *Living*

INTRODUCTION   IX

the Word Catholic Women's Bible to start reading about some of the women of scripture, our sisters in the faith. Or check out that Bible's Feature Index to follow a theme of interest through scripture. Sunday Mass readings can be found at usccb.org.

3. *Record your plan and chart your progress* on the Reading Log on pages xiii–xxii for later reference. Your log might look something like this:

GOAL	PROGRESS	JOURNAL PAGES
Sunday's readings	Dt 30:10–14, Ps 19:8–11	2–3
	Col 1:15-20	4–5
	Lk 10:25–37	6–7

4. *Read God's Word with a heart tuned to hear.* When you read, linger at places that are meaningful to you. As described in the *Living the Word Catholic Women's Bible's* "Where Do I Start?" feature (pages 1923–24): pray first, persist, ponder, and be patient. The scripture will nourish and transform you even if you can't feel it work. God wants to speak to you! The more you read, the more you'll learn to hear his voice.

You may not understand everything you read. That is okay. Focus on the things you do understand and take note of things you might want to explore further at a different time. The more familiar you become with scripture, particularly with the overall "story" of the Bible, and the more you deepen your knowledge of it and the Catholic faith through study, the richer your devotional reading will become. (For more about this, be sure to check out Catherine Cavadini's feature "Illuminating Fire" in the front of your Bible, pages xvii–xviii.)

Lord, thank you FOR THE GIFT OF SCRIPTURE. HELP ME TO GET TO KNOW YOU AND TO *hear you speak to my heart* AS I READ. GRANT THAT I MIGHT GROW IN FAITH AND LOVE OF YOU AND OTHERS AS I LEARN TO LIVE ACCORDING TO YOUR WORD. *Amen.*

Prayer before Reading Scripture

INTRODUCTION

5. *Journal as you read.* Begin by recording the date and passage you will read, then follow the prompts to write down your insights and questions as they occur to you. Copy down a meaningful verse in the space provided; the simple act of writing will help you internalize and remember it. Finally, write a short prayer in response to what you have read, including any way you feel prompted to "live the Word."

6. *Make your Bible your own.* As you read, don't be shy about underlining key words or highlighting phrases that are meaningful to you in your Bible. Use the margins to add insights or to note the date and occasion when a passage gave you strength or comfort or formed the basis of a prayer. Consider keeping a list of "life verses" you want to memorize in the back of your Bible for easy reference.

7. *Continue the conversation.* As you continue to ponder the truths of scripture, ask God to help you understand what you have read in a new way. Expect the Lord to speak to you throughout the day, revealing himself to you and showing you how to apply what you have read. Memorize important verses so they will come to mind when you need them. Record prayer intentions and things you're grateful for on pages 223–25, noting scripture that encourages or strengthens you regarding them, so you can look back and see how God has worked in your life.

8. *Finally, share your discoveries!* As you continue to explore the scriptures on your own, reading the insights of the women whose essays and other features you will find interspersed throughout the Bible text, consider inviting a few friends over for coffee to talk about what God has been saying to you in these daily encounters. Or join an established faith-sharing group at your parish. Talking and praying with your sisters in Christ, you may discover new insights into old questions and be inspired to return again and again to this well of living water you have discovered in the quiet of your home.

May God bless you as you read his Word!

Sarah Christmyer

General Editor
Living the Word Catholic Women's Bible

ONE GLANCE AT
the holy Gospel,
AND THE LIFE OF JESUS BECOMES A PERFUME THAT FILLS THE VERY AIR I BREATHE.

St. Thérèse of Lisieux

Reading Log

GOAL PROGRESS JOURNAL PAGES

GOAL	PROGRESS	JOURNAL PAGES

READING LOG

GOAL	PROGRESS	JOURNAL PAGES

GOAL	PROGRESS	JOURNAL PAGES

READING LOG

GOAL	PROGRESS	JOURNAL PAGES

| GOAL | PROGRESS | JOURNAL PAGES |

READING LOG   XIX

GOAL	PROGRESS	JOURNAL PAGES

GOAL	PROGRESS	JOURNAL PAGES

READING LOG XXI

GOAL	PROGRESS	JOURNAL PAGES

LIVING THE WORD COMPANION JOURNAL

| GOAL | PROGRESS | JOURNAL PAGES |

Journal Pages

100 Days in the Word

Today's Living Word

Date: _____

Today's Scripture Passage: _____

Key Verse

Notes and Observations:
(What does this say? What catches my attention? What do I not understand—or want to know more about?)

_____
_____
_____
_____
_____
_____
_____
_____

Going Deeper:
(How does this touch my life? What is God saying to me?)

_____
_____
_____
_____
_____
_____

My Prayer Response:
(How will I live this Word today?)

_____
_____
_____
_____
_____
_____

> SO FAITH, HOPE, LOVE ABIDE, THESE THREE; BUT THE GREATEST OF THESE IS LOVE.
>
> 1 Corinthians 13:13

Today's Living Word

Date:

Today's Scripture Passage:

— Key Verse —

Notes and Observations:
What does this say? What catches my attention? What do I not understand—or want to know more about?

Going Deeper:
(How does this touch my life? What is God saying to me?)

_____

_____

_____

_____

_____

My Prayer Response:
(How will I live this Word today?)

_____

_____

_____

_____

_____

> BE WATCHFUL, STAND FIRM IN YOUR FAITH, BE COURAGEOUS, BE STRONG. LET ALL THAT YOU DO BE DONE IN LOVE.
>
> 1 Corinthians 16:13-14

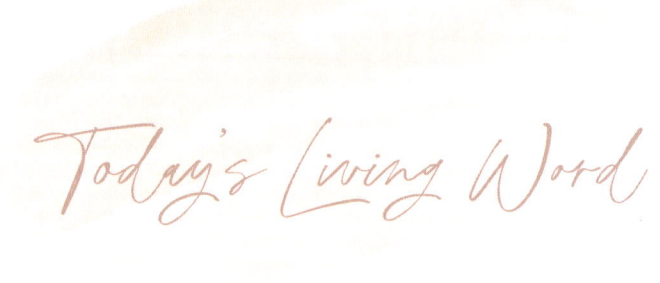

Date:

Today's Scripture Passage:

Key Verse

Notes and Observations:
(What does this say? What catches my attention? What do I not understand—or want to know more about?)

Going Deeper:

(How does this touch my life? What is God saying to me?)

_____
_____
_____
_____
_____
_____

My Prayer Response:

(How will I live this Word today?)

_____
_____
_____
_____
_____
_____

> SEEK FIRST HIS KINGDOM AND HIS RIGHTEOUSNESS, AND ALL THESE THINGS SHALL BE YOURS AS WELL.
>
> Matthew 6:33

Today's Living Word

Date:
_____

Today's Scripture Passage:
_____

— *Key Verse* —

Notes and Observations:
(What does this say? What catches my attention? What do I not understand—or want to know more about?)

_____

_____

_____

_____

_____

_____

_____

Going Deeper:
(How does this touch my life? What is God saying to me?)

_____

_____

_____

_____

_____

My Prayer Response:
(How will I live this Word today?)

_____

_____

_____

_____

_____

_____

> O TASTE AND SEE THAT THE LORD IS GOOD! BLESSED IS THE MAN WHO TAKES REFUGE IN HIM!
>
> Psalm 34:8

Today's Living Word

Date:

_____

Today's Scripture Passage:

_____

Key Verse

Notes and Observations:
(What does this say? What catches my attention? What do I not understand—or want to know more about?)

_____

_____

_____

_____

_____

_____

_____

_____

Going Deeper:

(How does this touch my life? What is God saying to me?)

_____
_____
_____
_____
_____

My Prayer Response:

(How will I live this Word today?)

_____
_____
_____
_____
_____

> I CONSIDER THAT THE SUFFERINGS OF THIS PRESENT TIME ARE NOT WORTH COMPARING WITH THE GLORY THAT IS TO BE REVEALED TO US.
>
> Romans 8:18

Today's Living Word

Date: _____

Today's Scripture Passage: _____

— *Key Verse* —

Notes and Observations:
(What does this say? What catches my attention? What do I not understand—or want to know more about?)

_____

_____

_____

_____

_____

_____

_____

_____

Going Deeper:
(How does this touch my life? What is God saying to me?)

_____
_____
_____
_____
_____

My Prayer Response:
(How will I live this Word today?)

_____
_____
_____
_____
_____

> THE LORD SEES NOT AS MAN SEES; MAN LOOKS ON THE OUTWARD APPEARANCE, BUT THE LORD LOOKS ON THE HEART.
>
> 1 Samuel 16:7

Today's Living Word

Date:
_____

Today's Scripture Passage:
_____

Key Verse

Notes and Observations:
(What does this say? What catches my attention? What do I not understand—or want to know more about?)

_____
_____
_____
_____
_____
_____
_____
_____

Going Deeper:
(How does this touch my life? What is God saying to me?)

_____

_____

_____

_____

_____

My Prayer Response:
(How will I live this Word today?)

_____

_____

_____

_____

> HE WHO BELIEVES IN ME, AS THE SCRIPTURE HAS SAID, "OUT OF HIS HEART SHALL FLOW RIVERS OF LIVING WATER."
>
> John 7:38

Today's Living Word

Date:

Today's Scripture Passage:

Key Verse

Notes and Observations:
(What does this say? What catches my attention? What do I not understand—or want to know more about?)

Going Deeper:
(How does this touch my life? What is God saying to me?)

_____
_____
_____
_____
_____
_____
_____

My Prayer Response:
(How will I live this Word today?)

_____
_____
_____
_____
_____
_____
_____

HE WHO CALLS YOU IS FAITHFUL, AND HE WILL DO IT.

1 Thessalonians 5:24

Today's Living Word

Date: _____

Today's Scripture Passage:

_____

Key Verse

Notes and Observations:
(What does this say? What catches my attention? What do I not understand—or want to know more about?)

_____

_____

_____

_____

_____

_____

_____

Going Deeper:
(How does this touch my life? What is God saying to me?)

_____

_____

_____

_____

_____

_____

_____

My Prayer Response:
(How will I live this Word today?)

_____

_____

_____

_____

_____

_____

> WHAT THEN SHALL WE SAY TO THIS? IF GOD IS FOR US, WHO IS AGAINST US?
>
> Romans 8:31

Today's Living Word

Date: _____

Today's Scripture Passage: _____

— Key Verse —

Notes and Observations:
(What does this say? What catches my attention? What do I not understand—or want to know more about?)

Going Deeper:
(How does this touch my life? What is God saying to me?)

My Prayer Response:
(How will I live this Word today?)

> THE FRUIT OF THE SPIRIT IS LOVE, JOY, PEACE, PATIENCE, KINDNESS, GOODNESS, FAITHFULNESS, GENTLENESS, SELF-CONTROL.
>
> Galatians 5:22-23

Taking Stock

EXAMINE YOURSELVES, TO SEE WHETHER YOU ARE HOLDING TO YOUR FAITH.

2 Corinthians 13:5

In the past ten days of journaling, the scripture that has meant most to me is:

My biggest aha moment was:

I learned this about God:

I am especially thankful for:

Lord, please help me to:

> It's important to note that God uses Esther's faith and courage to deliver her people *despite her fear*. All the fasting and prayer didn't change the fact that, even as she looked joyful before the king, her fear remained. . . . Fear like that isn't a sin, because it doesn't cause us to shrink away from doing what we know we must do. Fear can accompany faith, without replacing it.
>
> Gayle Somers,
> "Esther: Praying in Faith and Fear," page 664

Today's Living Word

Date:

_____

Today's Scripture Passage:

_____

— Key Verse —

Notes and Observations:
(What does this say? What catches my attention? What do I not understand—or want to know more about?)

_____

_____

_____

_____

_____

_____

_____

_____

Going Deeper:
(How does this touch my life? What is God saying to me?)

_____
_____
_____
_____
_____
_____
_____

My Prayer Response:
(How will I live this Word today?)

_____
_____
_____
_____
_____
_____
_____

> SURELY HE HAS BORNE OUR GRIEFS AND CARRIED OUR SORROWS.
>
> Isaiah 53:4

Today's Living Word

Date:

Today's Scripture Passage:

Key Verse

Notes and Observations:
(What does this say? What catches my attention? What do I not understand—or want to know more about?)

Going Deeper:

(How does this touch my life? What is God saying to me?)

_____
_____
_____
_____
_____
_____

My Prayer Response:

(How will I live this Word today?)

_____
_____
_____
_____
_____
_____

> BE FILLED WITH THE SPIRIT, ADDRESSING ONE ANOTHER IN PSALMS AND HYMNS AND SPIRITUAL SONGS.
>
> Ephesians 5:18-19

Today's Living Word

Date:

_____

Today's Scripture Passage:

_____

— *Key Verse* —

Notes and Observations:
(What does this say? What catches my attention? What do I not understand—or want to know more about?)

_____

_____

_____

_____

_____

_____

_____

_____

Going Deeper:
(How does this touch my life? What is God saying to me?)

_____
_____
_____
_____
_____

My Prayer Response:
(How will I live this Word today?)

_____
_____
_____
_____

> NOW FAITH IS THE ASSURANCE OF THINGS HOPED FOR, THE CONVICTION OF THINGS NOT SEEN.
>
> Hebrews 11:1

Date:

Today's Scripture Passage:

Key Verse

Notes and Observations:
(What does this say? What catches my attention? What do I not understand—or want to know more about?)

Going Deeper:
(How does this touch my life? What is God saying to me?)

_____
_____
_____
_____
_____
_____

My Prayer Response:
(How will I live this Word today?)

_____
_____
_____
_____
_____
_____

> MY SOUL MELTS AWAY FOR SORROW; STRENGTHEN ME ACCORDING TO YOUR WORD!
>
> Psalm 119:28

Today's Living Word

Date:

_____

Today's Scripture Passage:

_____

―― *Key Verse* ――

Notes and Observations:
(What does this say? What catches my attention? What do I not understand—or want to know more about?)

_____

_____

_____

_____

_____

_____

_____

Going Deeper:

(How does this touch my life? What is God saying to me?)

_____
_____
_____
_____
_____

My Prayer Response:

(How will I live this Word today?)

_____
_____
_____
_____
_____

> THE GRASS WITHERS, THE FLOWER FADES; BUT THE WORD OF OUR GOD WILL STAND FOR EVER.
>
> Isaiah 40:8

Today's Living Word

Date:
_____

Today's Scripture Passage:
_____

Key Verse

[   ]

Notes and Observations:
(What does this say? What catches my attention? What do I not understand—or want to know more about?)

_____

_____

_____

_____

_____

_____

_____

Going Deeper:

(How does this touch my life? What is God saying to me?)

_____
_____
_____
_____
_____
_____

My Prayer Response:

(How will I live this Word today?)

_____
_____
_____
_____
_____
_____

> BE STRONG AND OF GOOD COURAGE, DO NOT FEAR . . . FOR IT IS THE LORD YOUR GOD WHO GOES WITH YOU.
>
> Deuteronomy 31:6

Today's Living Word

Date:

Today's Scripture Passage:

――― Key Verse ―――

Notes and Observations:
(What does this say? What catches my attention? What do I not understand—or want to know more about?)

Going Deeper:
(How does this touch my life? What is God saying to me?)

_____
_____
_____
_____
_____
_____

My Prayer Response:
(How will I live this Word today?)

_____
_____
_____
_____
_____

> FOR WE ARE HIS WORKMANSHIP, CREATED IN CHRIST JESUS FOR GOOD WORKS, WHICH GOD PREPARED BEFOREHAND.
>
> Ephesians 2:10

Today's Living Word

Date:
_____

Today's Scripture Passage:
_____

Key Verse

Notes and Observations:
(What does this say? What catches my attention? What do I not understand—or want to know more about?)

_____
_____
_____
_____
_____
_____
_____

Going Deeper:
(How does this touch my life? What is God saying to me?)

_____
_____
_____
_____
_____

My Prayer Response:
(How will I live this Word today?)

_____
_____
_____
_____
_____

> WE KNOW THAT IN EVERYTHING GOD WORKS FOR GOOD WITH THOSE WHO LOVE HIM, WHO ARE CALLED ACCORDING TO HIS PURPOSE.
>
> Romans 8:28

Today's Living Word

Date: _____

Today's Scripture Passage: _____

--- *Key Verse* ---

Notes and Observations:
(What does this say? What catches my attention? What do I not understand—or want to know more about?)

_____
_____
_____
_____
_____
_____
_____
_____
_____

Going Deeper:
(How does this touch my life? What is God saying to me?)

My Prayer Response:
(How will I live this Word today?)

> MAY THE LORD DIRECT YOUR HEARTS TO THE LOVE OF GOD AND TO THE STEADFASTNESS OF CHRIST.
>
> 2 Thessalonians 3:5

Today's Living Word

Date: _____

Today's Scripture Passage: _____

— Key Verse —

Notes and Observations:
(What does this say? What catches my attention? What do I not understand—or want to know more about?)

_____

_____

_____

_____

_____

_____

_____

_____

Going Deeper:

(How does this touch my life? What is God saying to me?)

My Prayer Response:

(How will I live this Word today?)

> HEAL ME, O LORD, AND I SHALL BE HEALED; SAVE ME, AND I SHALL BE SAVED; FOR YOU ARE MY PRAISE.
>
> Jeremiah 17:14

EXAMINE YOURSELVES, TO SEE WHETHER YOU ARE HOLDING TO YOUR FAITH.

2 Corinthians 13:5

In the past ten days of journaling, the scripture that has meant most to me is:

_____

_____

_____

_____

My biggest aha moment was:

_____

_____

_____

I learned this about God:

_____

_____

I am especially thankful for:

Lord, please help me to:

It is our faith while we are in the desert that proves "God will supply every need" (Phil 4:19). The desert is meant to lead us into a relationship with him where we learn to draw strength, consolation, and provision. Once we have learned to rest in God, we have entered the promised land of Sabbath rest and plenitude.

Rest is a promise. Rest is a discipline.
Where do you need rest today?

Sonja Corbitt, "Made for Rest," pages 1492-93

Today's Living Word

Date:

Today's Scripture Passage:

Key Verse

Notes and Observations:
(What does this say? What catches my attention? What do I not understand—or want to know more about?)

Going Deeper:
(How does this touch my life? What is God saying to me?)

_____
_____
_____
_____
_____
_____

My Prayer Response:
(How will I live this Word today?)

_____
_____
_____
_____
_____
_____

> A NEW HEART I WILL GIVE YOU, AND A NEW SPIRIT I WILL PUT WITHIN YOU.
>
> Ezekiel 36:26

Today's Living Word

Date:
_____

Today's Scripture Passage:
_____

Key Verse

Notes and Observations:
(What does this say? What catches my attention? What do I not understand—or want to know more about?)

_____

_____

_____

_____

_____

_____

_____

Going Deeper:
(How does this touch my life? What is God saying to me?)

_____

_____

_____

_____

_____

_____

My Prayer Response:
(How will I live this Word today?)

_____

_____

_____

_____

_____

> JESUS THEN SAID . . .
> "IF YOU CONTINUE IN MY
> WORD, YOU ARE TRULY MY
> DISCIPLES, AND YOU WILL
> KNOW THE TRUTH."
>
> John 8:31

Today's Living Word

Date: _____

Today's Scripture Passage: _____

Key Verse

Notes and Observations:
(What does this say? What catches my attention? What do I not understand—or want to know more about?)

Going Deeper:
(How does this touch my life? What is God saying to me?)

_____
_____
_____
_____
_____
_____

My Prayer Response:
(How will I live this Word today?)

_____
_____
_____
_____
_____

> LEAD ME IN YOUR TRUTH, AND TEACH ME, FOR YOU ARE THE GOD OF MY SALVATION; FOR YOU I WAIT ALL THE DAY LONG.
>
> Psalm 25:5

Today's Living Word

Date: _____

Today's Scripture Passage: _____

Key Verse

Notes and Observations:
(What does this say? What catches my attention? What do I not understand—or want to know more about?)

_____

_____

_____

_____

_____

_____

_____

Going Deeper:

(How does this touch my life? What is God saying to me?)

_____

_____

_____

_____

_____

_____

My Prayer Response:

(How will I live this Word today?)

_____

_____

_____

_____

_____

> THE WORD OF GOD IS LIVING AND ACTIVE . . . DISCERNING THE THOUGHTS AND INTENTIONS OF THE HEART.
>
> Hebrews 4:12

Today's Living Word

Date: _____

Today's Scripture Passage: _____

Key Verse

Notes and Observations:
(What does this say? What catches my attention? What do I not understand—or want to know more about?)

_____

_____

_____

_____

_____

_____

_____

_____

Going Deeper:
(How does this touch my life? What is God saying to me?)

_____
_____
_____
_____
_____
_____

My Prayer Response:
(How will I live this Word today?)

_____
_____
_____
_____
_____
_____

> IF YOU ABIDE IN ME, AND MY WORDS ABIDE IN YOU, ASK WHATEVER YOU WILL, AND IT SHALL BE DONE FOR YOU.
>
> John 15:7

Today's Living Word

Date:

Today's Scripture Passage:

— Key Verse —

Notes and Observations:
(What does this say? What catches my attention? What do I not understand—or want to know more about?)

Going Deeper:
(How does this touch my life? What is God saying to me?)

_____

_____

_____

_____

_____

My Prayer Response:
(How will I live this Word today?)

_____

_____

_____

_____

_____

> COME, LET US RETURN TO THE LORD. . . . LET US KNOW, LET US PRESS ON TO KNOW THE LORD.
>
> Hosea 6:1, 3

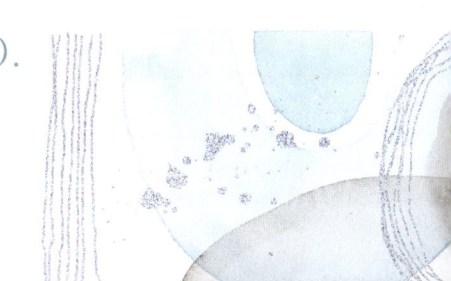

Today's Living Word

Date: _____

Today's Scripture Passage: _____

― *Key Verse* ―

Notes and Observations:
(What does this say? What catches my attention? What do I not understand—or want to know more about?)

_____

_____

_____

_____

_____

_____

_____

Going Deeper:
(How does this touch my life? What is God saying to me?)

_____
_____
_____
_____
_____

My Prayer Response:
(How will I live this Word today?)

_____
_____
_____
_____

> I KNOW THE PLANS I HAVE FOR YOU, SAYS THE LORD, PLANS FOR WELFARE AND NOT FOR EVIL, TO GIVE YOU A FUTURE AND A HOPE.
>
> Jeremiah 29:11

Today's Living Word

Date:

Today's Scripture Passage:

— Key Verse —

Notes and Observations:
(What does this say? What catches my attention? What do I not understand—or want to know more about?)

Going Deeper:

(How does this touch my life? What is God saying to me?)

My Prayer Response:

(How will I live this Word today?)

> ATTEND TO ME,
> AND ANSWER ME;
> I AM OVERCOME BY
> MY TROUBLE.
>
> Psalm 55:2

Today's Living Word

Date:

Today's Scripture Passage:

― Key Verse ―

Notes and Observations:
(What does this say? What catches my attention? What do I not understand—or want to know more about?)

Going Deeper:

(How does this touch my life? What is God saying to me?)

_____

_____

_____

_____

_____

_____

_____

My Prayer Response:

(How will I live this Word today?)

_____

_____

_____

_____

_____

_____

_____

> FEAR NOT, FOR I AM WITH YOU, BE NOT DISMAYED, FOR I AM YOUR GOD.
>
> Isaiah 41:10

Today's Living Word

Date:

_____

Today's Scripture Passage:

_____

Key Verse

Notes and Observations:
(What does this say? What catches my attention? What do I not understand—or want to know more about?)

_____
_____
_____
_____
_____
_____
_____
_____

Going Deeper:
(How does this touch my life? What is God saying to me?)

_____

_____

_____

_____

_____

_____

My Prayer Response:
(How will I live this Word today?)

_____

_____

_____

_____

_____

> BLESSED IS SHE WHO BELIEVED THAT THERE WOULD BE A FULFILMENT OF WHAT WAS SPOKEN TO HER FROM THE LORD.
>
> Luke 1:45

Taking Stock

EXAMINE YOURSELVES, TO SEE WHETHER YOU ARE HOLDING TO YOUR FAITH.

2 Corinthians 13:5

In the past ten days of journaling, the scripture that has meant most to me is:

My biggest aha moment was:

I learned this about God:

I am especially thankful for:

Lord, please help me to:

> In Baptism and Confirmation, we receive the same Holy Spirit who blazed among Christ's followers at Pentecost. How have I limited the Spirit's power by my own low expectations? *Come, Holy Spirit! Shape my life by the reading of God's Word!*
>
> Lavinia Spirito, "Take It to Heart"
> for the Acts of the Apostles, page 1705

Today's Living Word

Date:

Today's Scripture Passage:

Key Verse

Notes and Observations:
(What does this say? What catches my attention? What do I not understand—or want to know more about?)

Going Deeper:
(How does this touch my life? What is God saying to me?)

My Prayer Response:
(How will I live this Word today?)

> REJOICE IN YOUR HOPE, BE PATIENT IN TRIBULATION, BE CONSTANT IN PRAYER.
>
> Romans 12:12

Today's Living Word

Date: _____

Today's Scripture Passage: _____

Key Verse

Notes and Observations:
(What does this say? What catches my attention? What do I not understand—or want to know more about?)

_____
_____
_____
_____
_____
_____
_____
_____

Going Deeper:
(How does this touch my life? What is God saying to me?)

_____
_____
_____
_____
_____
_____

My Prayer Response:
(How will I live this Word today?)

_____
_____
_____
_____
_____
_____

> THE LORD IS MY SHEPHERD.
> ... HE LEADS ME BESIDE
> STILL WATERS; HE RESTORES
> MY SOUL.
>
> Psalm 23:1-3

Today's Living Word

Date:

Today's Scripture Passage:

Key Verse

Notes and Observations:
(What does this say? What catches my attention? What do I not understand—or want to know more about?)

Going Deeper:
(How does this touch my life? What is God saying to me?)

_____

_____

_____

_____

_____

My Prayer Response:
(How will I live this Word today?)

_____

_____

_____

_____

_____

> THE STEADFAST LOVE OF
> THE LORD NEVER CEASES,
> HIS MERCIES NEVER COME
> TO AN END; THEY ARE
> NEW EVERY MORNING.
>
> Lamentations 3:22-23

Today's Living Word

Date: _____

Today's Scripture Passage: _____

Key Verse

Notes and Observations:
(What does this say? What catches my attention? What do I not understand—or want to know more about?)

Going Deeper:
(How does this touch my life? What is God saying to me?)

_____
_____
_____
_____
_____
_____

My Prayer Response:
(How will I live this Word today?)

_____
_____
_____
_____
_____
_____

> TRAIN UP A CHILD IN THE WAY HE SHOULD GO, AND WHEN HE IS OLD HE WILL NOT DEPART FROM IT.
>
> Proverbs 22:6

Today's Living Word

Date:

_____

Today's Scripture Passage:

_____

Key Verse

Notes and Observations:
(What does this say? What catches my attention? What do I not understand—or want to know more about?)

_____

_____

_____

_____

_____

_____

_____

_____

Going Deeper:
(How does this touch my life? What is God saying to me?)

My Prayer Response:
(How will I live this Word today?)

> RETURN TO ME, SAYS THE LORD OF HOSTS, AND I WILL RETURN TO YOU.
>
> Zechariah 1:3

Date:
_____

Today's Scripture Passage:
_____

Key Verse

Notes and Observations:
(What does this say? What catches my attention? What do I not understand—or want to know more about?)

_____
_____
_____
_____
_____
_____
_____

Going Deeper:
(How does this touch my life? What is God saying to me?)

My Prayer Response:
(How will I live this Word today?)

> LET NOT YOUR HEARTS
> BE TROUBLED; BELIEVE IN
> GOD, BELIEVE ALSO
> IN ME.
>
> John 14:1

Today's Living Word

Date:

Today's Scripture Passage:

Key Verse

Notes and Observations:
(What does this say? What catches my attention? What do I not understand—or want to know more about?)

Going Deeper:
(How does this touch my life? What is God saying to me?)

_____
_____
_____
_____
_____
_____
_____

My Prayer Response:
(How will I live this Word today?)

_____
_____
_____
_____
_____
_____

> THERE IS GREAT GAIN
> IN GODLINESS WITH
> CONTENTMENT.
>
> 1 Timothy 6:6

Today's Living Word

Date: _____

Today's Scripture Passage:
_____

— Key Verse —

Notes and Observations:
(What does this say? What catches my attention? What do I not understand—or want to know more about?)

Going Deeper:
(How does this touch my life? What is God saying to me?)

_____
_____
_____
_____
_____
_____

My Prayer Response:
(How will I live this Word today?)

_____
_____
_____
_____
_____
_____

> PEACE I LEAVE WITH YOU;
> MY PEACE I GIVE TO YOU;
> NOT AS THE WORLD GIVES
> DO I GIVE TO YOU.
>
> John 14:27

Today's Living Word

Date:

_____

Today's Scripture Passage:

_____

---- *Key Verse* ----

Notes and Observations:

(What does this say? What catches my attention? What do I not understand—or want to know more about?)

_____

_____

_____

_____

_____

_____

_____

Going Deeper:
(How does this touch my life? What is God saying to me?)

_____
_____
_____
_____
_____
_____

My Prayer Response:
(How will I live this Word today?)

_____
_____
_____
_____
_____
_____

> I PRAISE YOU, FOR
> I AM WONDROUSLY
> MADE. WONDERFUL ARE
> YOUR WORKS!
>
> Psalm 139:14

Today's Living Word

Date: _____

Today's Scripture Passage: _____

--- *Key Verse* ---

Notes and Observations:
(What does this say? What catches my attention? What do I not understand—or want to know more about?)

_____
_____
_____
_____
_____
_____
_____

Going Deeper:
(How does this touch my life? What is God saying to me?)

_____
_____
_____
_____
_____
_____

My Prayer Response:
(How will I live this Word today?)

_____
_____
_____
_____
_____
_____

> GIVE ME UNDERSTANDING,
> THAT I MAY KEEP YOUR LAW
> AND OBSERVE IT WITH MY
> WHOLE HEART.
>
> Psalm 119:34

EXAMINE YOURSELVES, TO SEE WHETHER YOU ARE HOLDING TO YOUR FAITH.

2 Corinthians 13:5

In the past ten days of journaling, the scripture that has meant most to me is:

___

___

___

My biggest aha moment was:

___

___

___

I learned this about God:

___

___

I am especially thankful for:

Lord, please help me to:

> How are we to remain safe in a world that doesn't even acknowledge that the devil exists? In Ephesians 6:10-20 Paul gives us our instructions for battle.... We must match [the devil's] persistence with our prayer.
>
> Sandy Wanzeck,
> "Put On Your Armor!" page 1784

Today's Living Word

Date: _____

Today's Scripture Passage: _____

— *Key Verse* —

Notes and Observations:
(What does this say? What catches my attention? What do I not understand—or want to know more about?)

Going Deeper:

(How does this touch my life? What is God saying to me?)

___

___

___

___

___

___

___

My Prayer Response:

(How will I live this Word today?)

___

___

___

___

___

___

___

> IN THE WORLD YOU HAVE
> TRIBULATION; BUT BE
> OF GOOD CHEER, I HAVE
> OVERCOME THE WORLD.
>
> John 16:33

Today's Living Word

Date:

_____

Today's Scripture Passage:

_____

— *Key Verse* —

Notes and Observations:
(What does this say? What catches my attention? What do I not understand—or want to know more about?)

Going Deeper:
(How does this touch my life? What is God saying to me?)

My Prayer Response:
(How will I live this Word today?)

> I WAIT FOR THE LORD,
> MY SOUL WAITS, AND IN
> HIS WORD I HOPE.
>
> Psalm 130:5

Today's Living Word

Date:

Today's Scripture Passage:

Key Verse

Notes and Observations:
(What does this say? What catches my attention? What do I not understand—or want to know more about?)

Going Deeper:
(How does this touch my life? What is God saying to me?)

My Prayer Response:
(How will I live this Word today?)

> CHOOSE THIS DAY WHOM YOU WILL SERVE . . . ; BUT AS FOR ME AND MY HOUSE, WE WILL SERVE THE LORD.
>
> Joshua 24:15

Today's Living Word

Date: _____

Today's Scripture Passage:
_____

— *Key Verse* —

Notes and Observations:
(What does this say? What catches my attention? What do I not understand—or want to know more about?)

Going Deeper:

(How does this touch my life? What is God saying to me?)

___

___

___

___

___

___

___

My Prayer Response:

(How will I live this Word today?)

___

___

___

___

___

___

> YOUR WORD IS A LAMP TO MY FEET AND A LIGHT TO MY PATH.
>
> Psalm 119:105

Today's Living Word

Date: _____

Today's Scripture Passage: _____

Key Verse

Notes and Observations:
(What does this say? What catches my attention? What do I not understand—or want to know more about?)

_____
_____
_____
_____
_____
_____
_____
_____

Going Deeper:
(How does this touch my life? What is God saying to me?)

_____

_____

_____

_____

_____

_____

My Prayer Response:
(How will I live this Word today?)

_____

_____

_____

_____

_____

> IF ANY ONE IS IN CHRIST,
> HE IS A NEW CREATION;
> THE OLD HAS PASSED AWAY,
> BEHOLD, THE NEW
> HAS COME.
>
> 2 Corinthians 5:17

Today's Living Word

Date: _____

Today's Scripture Passage: _____

――― *Key Verse* ―――

Notes and Observations:
(What does this say? What catches my attention? What do I not understand—or want to know more about?)

Going Deeper:
(How does this touch my life? What is God saying to me?)

My Prayer Response:
(How will I live this Word today?)

> YOU SHALL LOVE THE LORD YOUR GOD WITH ALL YOUR HEART, AND WITH ALL YOUR SOUL, AND WITH ALL YOUR MIND, AND WITH ALL YOUR STRENGTH.
>
> Mark 12:30

Today's Living Word

Date:

_____

Today's Scripture Passage:

_____

Key Verse

Notes and Observations:

(What does this say? What catches my attention? What do I not understand—or want to know more about?)

_____

_____

_____

_____

_____

_____

_____

_____

Going Deeper:
(How does this touch my life? What is God saying to me?)

My Prayer Response:
(How will I live this Word today?)

> THEY WHO WAIT FOR THE LORD SHALL RENEW THEIR STRENGTH.
>
> Isaiah 40:31

Today's Living Word

Date:
_____

Today's Scripture Passage:
_____

Key Verse

Notes and Observations:
(What does this say? What catches my attention? What do I not understand—or want to know more about?)

_____
_____
_____
_____
_____
_____
_____

Going Deeper:
(How does this touch my life? What is God saying to me?)

_____
_____
_____
_____
_____
_____

My Prayer Response:
(How will I live this Word today?)

_____
_____
_____
_____
_____
_____

> BUT LOVE YOUR ENEMIES, AND DO GOOD, AND LEND, EXPECTING NOTHING IN RETURN; AND YOUR REWARD WILL BE GREAT.
>
> Luke 6:35

Today's Living Word

Date:

Today's Scripture Passage:

Key Verse

Notes and Observations:
(What does this say? What catches my attention? What do I not understand—or want to know more about?)

Going Deeper:
(How does this touch my life? What is God saying to me?)

_____

_____

_____

_____

_____

_____

_____

My Prayer Response:
(How will I live this Word today?)

_____

_____

_____

_____

_____

_____

> GOD IS OUR REFUGE AND STRENGTH, A VERY PRESENT HELP IN TROUBLE.
>
> Psalm 46:1

Today's Living Word

Date:

Today's Scripture Passage:

Key Verse

Notes and Observations:
(What does this say? What catches my attention? What do I not understand—or want to know more about?)

Going Deeper:
(How does this touch my life? What is God saying to me?)

My Prayer Response:
(How will I live this Word today?)

> BLESSED RATHER ARE THOSE WHO HEAR THE WORD OF GOD AND KEEP IT!
>
> Luke 11:28

EXAMINE YOURSELVES, TO SEE WHETHER YOU ARE HOLDING TO YOUR FAITH.

2 Corinthians 13:5

In the past ten days of journaling, the scripture that has meant most to me is:

My biggest aha moment was:

I learned this about God:

I am especially thankful for:

Lord, please help me to:

"I believe; help my unbelief!" (Mk 9:24).

Throughout Mark's gospel, the humanity of the Twelve struggling to have faith in Jesus reassures us that the smallest mustard seed of faith is enough. Jesus provides the rest!

Colleen Reiss Vermeulen,
Introduction to the Gospel of Mark,
page 1527

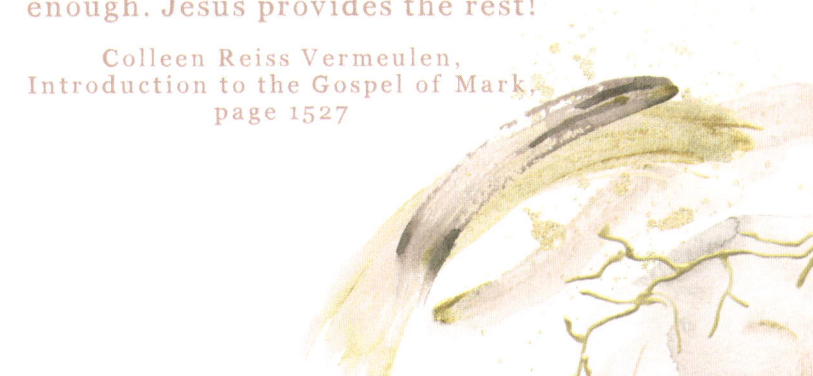

Today's Living Word

Date:

Today's Scripture Passage:

Key Verse

Notes and Observations:
(What does this say? What catches my attention? What do I not understand—or want to know more about?)

Going Deeper:
(How does this touch my life? What is God saying to me?)

_____
_____
_____
_____
_____

My Prayer Response:
(How will I live this Word today?)

_____
_____
_____
_____
_____

> REPENT THEREFORE, AND TURN AGAIN, . . . THAT TIMES OF REFRESHING MAY COME FROM THE PRESENCE OF THE LORD.
>
> Acts 3:19

Today's Living Word

Date: _____

Today's Scripture Passage: _____

Key Verse

Notes and Observations:
(What does this say? What catches my attention? What do I not understand—or want to know more about?)

_____
_____
_____
_____
_____
_____
_____

Going Deeper:
(How does this touch my life? What is God saying to me?)

_____
_____
_____
_____
_____
_____
_____
_____

My Prayer Response:
(How will I live this Word today?)

_____
_____
_____
_____
_____
_____
_____

> I HAVE LAID UP YOUR WORD IN MY HEART, THAT I MIGHT NOT SIN AGAINST YOU.
>
> Psalm 119:11

Today's Living Word

Date: _____

Today's Scripture Passage: _____

―――― *Key Verse* ――――

Notes and Observations:
(What does this say? What catches my attention? What do I not understand—or want to know more about?)

_____

_____

_____

_____

_____

_____

_____

Going Deeper:

(How does this touch my life? What is God saying to me?)

_____
_____
_____
_____
_____
_____

My Prayer Response:

(How will I live this Word today?)

_____
_____
_____
_____
_____

> MAN SHALL NOT LIVE BY BREAD ALONE, BUT BY EVERY WORD THAT PROCEEDS FROM THE MOUTH OF GOD.
>
> Matthew 4:4

Today's Living Word

Date:

_____

Today's Scripture Passage:

_____

Key Verse

Notes and Observations:
(What does this say? What catches my attention? What do I not understand—or want to know more about?)

_____
_____
_____
_____
_____
_____
_____
_____

Going Deeper:
(How does this touch my life? What is God saying to me?)

_____

_____

_____

_____

_____

_____

My Prayer Response:
(How will I live this Word today?)

_____

_____

_____

_____

_____

_____

> I AM THE WAY, AND THE TRUTH, AND THE LIFE; NO ONE COMES TO THE FATHER, BUT BY ME.
>
> John 14:6

Today's Living Word

Date:

_____

Today's Scripture Passage:

_____

Key Verse

Notes and Observations:
(What does this say? What catches my attention? What do I not understand—or want to know more about?)

_____
_____
_____
_____
_____
_____
_____
_____

Going Deeper:
(How does this touch my life? What is God saying to me?)

_____
_____
_____
_____
_____
_____

My Prayer Response:
(How will I live this Word today?)

_____
_____
_____
_____
_____
_____

> BE CONTENT WITH WHAT YOU HAVE; FOR HE HAS SAID, "I WILL NEVER FAIL YOU NOR FORSAKE YOU."
>
> Hebrews 13:5

Today's Living Word

Date: _____

Today's Scripture Passage: _____

--- Key Verse ---

Notes and Observations:
(What does this say? What catches my attention? What do I not understand—or want to know more about?)

_____

_____

_____

_____

_____

_____

_____

Going Deeper:
(How does this touch my life? What is God saying to me?)

_____

_____

_____

_____

_____

My Prayer Response:
(How will I live this Word today?)

_____

_____

_____

_____

_____

> EVERY ONE THEN WHO HEARS THESE WORDS OF MINE AND DOES THEM WILL BE LIKE A WISE MAN WHO BUILT HIS HOUSE UPON THE ROCK.
>
> Matthew 7:24

Today's Living Word

Date: _____

Today's Scripture Passage:
_____

Key Verse

Notes and Observations:
(What does this say? What catches my attention? What do I not understand—or want to know more about?)

Going Deeper:
(How does this touch my life? What is God saying to me?)

_____
_____
_____
_____
_____
_____

My Prayer Response:
(How will I live this Word today?)

_____
_____
_____
_____

> YOU HAVE TURNED MY MOURNING INTO DANCING; YOU HAVE LOOSED MY SACKCLOTH AND CLOTHED ME WITH GLADNESS.
>
> Psalm 30:11

Today's Living Word

Date:

_____

Today's Scripture Passage:

_____

— *Key Verse* —

Notes and Observations:
(What does this say? What catches my attention? What do I not understand—or want to know more about?)

_____
_____
_____
_____
_____
_____
_____
_____

Going Deeper:

(How does this touch my life? What is God saying to me?)

_____

_____

_____

_____

_____

_____

My Prayer Response:

(How will I live this Word today?)

_____

_____

_____

_____

_____

> ABOVE ALL HOLD UNFAILING YOUR LOVE FOR ONE ANOTHER, SINCE LOVE COVERS A MULTITUDE OF SINS.
>
> 1 Peter 4:8

Today's Living Word

Date:

Today's Scripture Passage:

Key Verse

Notes and Observations:
(What does this say? What catches my attention? What do I not understand—or want to know more about?)

Going Deeper:

(How does this touch my life? What is God saying to me?)

My Prayer Response:

(How will I live this Word today?)

> MAY MERCY, PEACE, AND LOVE BE MULTIPLIED TO YOU.
>
> Jude 1:2

Today's Living Word

Date: _____

Today's Scripture Passage:
_____

Key Verse

Notes and Observations:
(What does this say? What catches my attention? What do I not understand—or want to know more about?)

_____
_____
_____
_____
_____
_____
_____

Going Deeper:
(How does this touch my life? What is God saying to me?)

_____

_____

_____

_____

_____

My Prayer Response:
(How will I live this Word today?)

_____

_____

_____

_____

_____

> THE LORD IS GOOD, A STRONGHOLD IN THE DAY OF TROUBLE; HE KNOWS THOSE WHO TAKE REFUGE IN HIM.
>
> Nahum 1:7

EXAMINE YOURSELVES, TO SEE WHETHER YOU ARE HOLDING TO YOUR FAITH.

2 Corinthians 13:5

In the past ten days of journaling, the scripture that has meant most to me is:

My biggest aha moment was:

I learned this about God:

I am especially thankful for:

Lord, please help me to:

> God is love—in his being, in his very essence. His love is rich and full of compassion, grace, faithfulness, and mercy.
>
> Once we come to understand this great foundational truth, we will spend the rest of our lives showing God's mercy to others through compassion and service.
>
> Martha Fernandez-Sardina,
> "God Is Love," page 1887

Today's Living Word

Date: _____

Today's Scripture Passage: _____

— Key Verse —

Notes and Observations:
(What does this say? What catches my attention? What do I not understand—or want to know more about?)

_____
_____
_____
_____
_____
_____
_____
_____

Going Deeper:
(How does this touch my life? What is God saying to me?)

_____

_____

_____

_____

_____

_____

My Prayer Response:
(How will I live this Word today?)

_____

_____

_____

_____

_____

_____

> WALK IN A MANNER WORTHY OF THE CALLING TO WHICH YOU HAVE BEEN CALLED.
>
> Ephesians 4:1

Today's Living Word

Date:

Today's Scripture Passage:

―― Key Verse ――

Notes and Observations:
(What does this say? What catches my attention? What do I not understand—or want to know more about?)

Going Deeper:
(How does this touch my life? What is God saying to me?)

_____

_____

_____

_____

_____

_____

_____

My Prayer Response:
(How will I live this Word today?)

_____

_____

_____

_____

_____

_____

_____

> I CAN DO ALL THINGS
> IN HIM WHO
> STRENGTHENS ME.
>
> Philippians 4:13

Today's Living Word

Date: _____

Today's Scripture Passage: _____

Key Verse

Notes and Observations:
(What does this say? What catches my attention? What do I not understand—or want to know more about?)

Going Deeper:
(How does this touch my life? What is God saying to me?)

___

My Prayer Response:
(How will I live this Word today?)

___

> DO NOT BE GRIEVED, FOR
> THE JOY OF THE LORD IS
> YOUR STRENGTH.
>
> Nehemiah 8:10

Today's Living Word

Date:

Today's Scripture Passage:

Key Verse

Notes and Observations:
(What does this say? What catches my attention? What do I not understand—or want to know more about?)

Going Deeper:
(How does this touch my life? What is God saying to me?)

My Prayer Response:
(How will I live this Word today?)

> FOR THE LORD GIVES WISDOM; FROM HIS MOUTH COME KNOWLEDGE AND UNDERSTANDING.
>
> Proverbs 2:6

Date:

Today's Scripture Passage:

— Key Verse —

Notes and Observations:
(What does this say? What catches my attention? What do I not understand—or want to know more about?)

Going Deeper:

(How does this touch my life? What is God saying to me?)

My Prayer Response:

(How will I live this Word today?)

> FOR GOD DID NOT GIVE US A SPIRIT OF TIMIDITY BUT A SPIRIT OF POWER AND LOVE AND SELF-CONTROL.
>
> 2 Timothy 1:7

Today's Living Word

Date:

Today's Scripture Passage:

Key Verse

Notes and Observations:
(What does this say? What catches my attention? What do I not understand—or want to know more about?)

Going Deeper:
(How does this touch my life? What is God saying to me?)

My Prayer Response:
(How will I live this Word today?)

> THE SOULS OF THE RIGHTEOUS ARE IN THE HAND OF GOD, AND NO TORMENT WILL EVER TOUCH THEM.
>
> Wisdom 3:1

Today's Living Word

Date:
_____

Today's Scripture Passage:
_____

Key Verse

Notes and Observations:
(What does this say? What catches my attention? What do I not understand—or want to know more about?)

_____

_____

_____

_____

_____

_____

_____

Going Deeper:
(How does this touch my life? What is God saying to me?)

My Prayer Response:
(How will I live this Word today?)

> MY GOD WILL SUPPLY EVERY NEED OF YOURS ACCORDING TO HIS RICHES IN GLORY IN CHRIST JESUS.
>
> Philippians 4:19

Today's Living Word

Date:

Today's Scripture Passage:

Key Verse

Notes and Observations:
(What does this say? What catches my attention? What do I not understand—or want to know more about?)

Going Deeper:
(How does this touch my life? What is God saying to me?)

_____
_____
_____
_____
_____
_____
_____

My Prayer Response:
(How will I live this Word today?)

_____
_____
_____
_____
_____
_____
_____

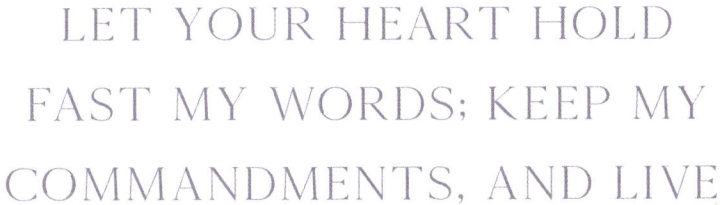

LET YOUR HEART HOLD FAST MY WORDS; KEEP MY COMMANDMENTS, AND LIVE.

Proverbs 4:4

Today's Living Word

Date:

Today's Scripture Passage:

Key Verse

Notes and Observations:
(What does this say? What catches my attention? What do I not understand—or want to know more about?)

Going Deeper:
(How does this touch my life? What is God saying to me?)

_____
_____
_____
_____
_____

My Prayer Response:
(How will I live this Word today?)

_____
_____
_____
_____
_____

> BE STRONG AND OF GOOD COURAGE; BE NOT FRIGHTENED, NEITHER BE DISMAYED; FOR THE LORD YOUR GOD IS WITH YOU WHEREVER YOU GO.
>
> Joshua 1:9

Today's Living Word

Date:

Today's Scripture Passage:

Key Verse

Notes and Observations:
(What does this say? What catches my attention? What do I not understand—or want to know more about?)

Going Deeper:

(How does this touch my life? What is God saying to me?)

My Prayer Response:

(How will I live this Word today?)

> THE LORD IS MY STRENGTH AND MY SHIELD; IN HIM MY HEART TRUSTS.
>
> Psalm 28:7

Taking Stock

EXAMINE YOURSELVES, TO SEE WHETHER YOU ARE HOLDING TO YOUR FAITH.

2 Corinthians 13:5

In the past ten days of journaling, the scripture that has meant most to me is:

My biggest aha moment was:

I learned this about God:

I am especially thankful for:

Lord, please help me to:

> God wants to speak to you! Hearing him is his desire for us all. But we need to get quiet, to still our own interior noise, and lean in to hear that still, small voice above the din of the world.
>
> Barbara Heil,
> "Listening for the Voice of God," page 468

Today's Living Word

Date:

Today's Scripture Passage:

Key Verse

Notes and Observations:
(What does this say? What catches my attention? What do I not understand—or want to know more about?)

Going Deeper:
(How does this touch my life? What is God saying to me?)

My Prayer Response:
(How will I live this Word today?)

> FOR WITH GOD NOTHING WILL BE IMPOSSIBLE.
>
> Luke 1:37

Today's Living Word

Date: _____

Today's Scripture Passage: _____

— *Key Verse* —

Notes and Observations:
(What does this say? What catches my attention? What do I not understand—or want to know more about?)

Going Deeper:

(How does this touch my life? What is God saying to me?)

My Prayer Response:

(How will I live this Word today?)

> I SOUGHT THE LORD,
> AND HE ANSWERED ME, AND
> DELIVERED ME FROM ALL MY
> FEARS.
>
> Psalm 34:4

Today's Living Word

Date:

Today's Scripture Passage:

Key Verse

Notes and Observations:
(What does this say? What catches my attention? What do I not understand—or want to know more about?)

Going Deeper:
(How does this touch my life? What is God saying to me?)

_____
_____
_____
_____
_____

My Prayer Response:
(How will I live this Word today?)

_____
_____
_____
_____
_____

> ALL SCRIPTURE IS INSPIRED
> BY GOD AND PROFITABLE
> FOR TEACHING, FOR
> REPROOF, FOR CORRECTION,
> AND FOR TRAINING
> IN RIGHTEOUSNESS.
>
> 2 Timothy 3:16

Today's Living Word

Date:

Today's Scripture Passage:

Key Verse

Notes and Observations:
(What does this say? What catches my attention? What do I not understand—or want to know more about?)

Going Deeper:

(How does this touch my life? What is God saying to me?)

_____

_____

_____

_____

_____

_____

My Prayer Response:

(How will I live this Word today?)

_____

_____

_____

_____

_____

_____

> WHEN THE CARES OF MY
> HEART ARE MANY,
> YOUR CONSOLATIONS
> CHEER MY SOUL.
>
> Psalm 94:19

Today's Living Word

Date:

Today's Scripture Passage:

Key Verse

Notes and Observations:
(What does this say? What catches my attention? What do I not understand—or want to know more about?)

Going Deeper:
(How does this touch my life? What is God saying to me?)

_____
_____
_____
_____
_____
_____
_____

My Prayer Response:
(How will I live this Word today?)

_____
_____
_____
_____
_____
_____
_____

> BLESSED ARE THE MERCIFUL,
> FOR THEY SHALL OBTAIN
> MERCY.
>
> Matthew 5:7

Today's Living Word

Date: _____

Today's Scripture Passage: _____

Key Verse

Notes and Observations:
(What does this say? What catches my attention? What do I not understand—or want to know more about?)

_____
_____
_____
_____
_____
_____
_____

Going Deeper:
(How does this touch my life? What is God saying to me?)

_____
_____
_____
_____
_____
_____
_____

My Prayer Response:
(How will I live this Word today?)

_____
_____
_____
_____
_____
_____
_____

> OPEN MY EYES, THAT I MAY BEHOLD WONDROUS THINGS OUT OF YOUR LAW.
>
> Psalm 119:18

Today's Living Word

Date:

Today's Scripture Passage:

Key Verse

Notes and Observations:
(What does this say? What catches my attention? What do I not understand—or want to know more about?)

Going Deeper:
(How does this touch my life? What is God saying to me?)

My Prayer Response:
(How will I live this Word today?)

BE DOERS OF THE WORD,
AND NOT HEARERS ONLY,
DECEIVING YOURSELVES.

James 1:22

Today's Living Word

Date: _____

Today's Scripture Passage: _____

Key Verse

Notes and Observations:
(What does this say? What catches my attention? What do I not understand—or want to know more about?)

Going Deeper:
(How does this touch my life? What is God saying to me?)

_____
_____
_____
_____
_____

My Prayer Response:
(How will I live this Word today?)

_____
_____
_____
_____

> TAKE MY YOKE UPON YOU, AND LEARN FROM ME; FOR I AM GENTLE AND LOWLY IN HEART, AND YOU WILL FIND REST FOR YOUR SOULS.
>
> Matthew 11:29

Today's Living Word

Date: _____

Today's Scripture Passage: _____

--- *Key Verse* ---

Notes and Observations:
(What does this say? What catches my attention? What do I not understand—or want to know more about?)

_____

_____

_____

_____

_____

_____

_____

Going Deeper:

(How does this touch my life? What is God saying to me?)

_____
_____
_____
_____
_____

My Prayer Response:

(How will I live this Word today?)

_____
_____
_____
_____
_____

> AND MARY SAID, "MY SOUL MAGNIFIES THE LORD . . . FOR HE WHO IS MIGHTY HAS DONE GREAT THINGS FOR ME, AND HOLY IS HIS NAME."
>
> Luke 1:46-49

Today's Living Word

Date:

Today's Scripture Passage:

Key Verse

Notes and Observations:
(What does this say? What catches my attention? What do I not understand—or want to know more about?)

Going Deeper:
(How does this touch my life? What is God saying to me?)

_____
_____
_____
_____
_____
_____

My Prayer Response:
(How will I live this Word today?)

_____
_____
_____
_____
_____
_____

> SEARCH ME, O GOD, AND KNOW MY HEART! TRY ME AND KNOW MY THOUGHTS!
>
> Psalm 139:23

EXAMINE YOURSELVES, TO SEE WHETHER YOU ARE HOLDING TO YOUR FAITH.

2 Corinthians 13:5

In the past ten days of journaling, the scripture that has meant most to me is:

My biggest aha moment was:

I learned this about God:

I am especially thankful for:

Lord, please help me to:

> Growing in faith means not only coming to a deeper knowledge and understanding but living in a way that is more fully committed to God. Growing in hope in God's promise of eternal life leads us to greater trust in and reliance on God. And growing in charity inspires and gives life to all other virtues; without it the most brilliant defense of the faith is merely a noisy gong (1 Cor 13:1).
>
> Ashley Crane,
> Introduction to the Letter of Jude, page 1895

Today's Living Word

Date: _____

Today's Scripture Passage: _____

Key Verse

Notes and Observations:
(What does this say? What catches my attention? What do I not understand—or want to know more about?)

_____
_____
_____
_____
_____
_____
_____
_____

Going Deeper:
(How does this touch my life? What is God saying to me?)

My Prayer Response:
(How will I live this Word today?)

> I WILL BLESS THE LORD AT ALL TIMES; HIS PRAISE SHALL CONTINUALLY BE IN MY MOUTH.
>
> Psalm 34:1

Today's Living Word

Date: _____

Today's Scripture Passage: _____

Key Verse

Notes and Observations:

(What does this say? What catches my attention? What do I not understand—or want to know more about?)

Going Deeper:
(How does this touch my life? What is God saying to me?)

_____
_____
_____
_____
_____
_____
_____
_____

My Prayer Response:
(How will I live this Word today?)

_____
_____
_____
_____
_____
_____
_____
_____

> CAST ALL YOUR ANXIETIES ON HIM, FOR HE CARES ABOUT YOU.
>
> 1 Peter 5:7

Today's Living Word

Date:

Today's Scripture Passage:

Key Verse

Notes and Observations:
(What does this say? What catches my attention? What do I not understand—or want to know more about?)

Going Deeper:
(How does this touch my life? What is God saying to me?)

_____

_____

_____

_____

_____

_____

My Prayer Response:
(How will I live this Word today?)

_____

_____

_____

_____

_____

> GOD . . . WILL NOT LET YOU BE TEMPTED BEYOND YOUR STRENGTH, BUT [WILL] PROVIDE THE WAY OF ESCAPE.
>
> 1 Corinthians 10:13

Today's Living Word

Date: _____

Today's Scripture Passage: _____

--- Key Verse ---

Notes and Observations:
(What does this say? What catches my attention? What do I not understand—or want to know more about?)

Going Deeper:
(How does this touch my life? What is God saying to me?)

_____

_____

_____

_____

_____

_____

_____

My Prayer Response:
(How will I live this Word today?)

_____

_____

_____

_____

_____

_____

_____

> TRUST IN THE LORD WITH ALL YOUR HEART, AND DO NOT RELY ON YOUR OWN INSIGHT.
>
> Proverbs 3:5

Today's Living Word

Date:

Today's Scripture Passage:

— Key Verse —

Notes and Observations:
(What does this say? What catches my attention? What do I not understand—or want to know more about?)

Going Deeper:
(How does this touch my life? What is God saying to me?)

_____
_____
_____
_____
_____
_____
_____

My Prayer Response:
(How will I live this Word today?)

_____
_____
_____
_____
_____
_____
_____

> HEAVEN AND EARTH WILL PASS AWAY, BUT MY WORDS WILL NOT PASS AWAY.
>
> Matthew 24:35

Today's Living Word

Date:

Today's Scripture Passage:

Key Verse

Notes and Observations:
(What does this say? What catches my attention? What do I not understand—or want to know more about?)

Going Deeper:

(How does this touch my life? What is God saying to me?)

My Prayer Response:

(How will I live this Word today?)

> THEREFORE ENCOURAGE ONE ANOTHER AND BUILD ONE ANOTHER UP, JUST AS YOU ARE DOING.
>
> 1 Thessalonians 5:11

Today's Living Word

Date:

Today's Scripture Passage:

Key Verse

Notes and Observations:
(What does this say? What catches my attention? What do I not understand—or want to know more about?)

Going Deeper:

(How does this touch my life? What is God saying to me?)

_____
_____
_____
_____
_____
_____

My Prayer Response:

(How will I live this Word today?)

_____
_____
_____
_____
_____
_____

> FINALLY, BE STRONG IN THE LORD AND IN THE STRENGTH OF HIS MIGHT.
>
> Ephesians 6:10

Today's Living Word

Date:

Today's Scripture Passage:

Key Verse

Notes and Observations:
(What does this say? What catches my attention? What do I not understand—or want to know more about?)

Going Deeper:
(How does this touch my life? What is God saying to me?)

_____
_____
_____
_____
_____
_____

My Prayer Response:
(How will I live this Word today?)

_____
_____
_____
_____
_____

> TEACH ME YOUR WAY,
> O LORD, THAT I MAY WALK
> IN YOUR TRUTH; UNITE
> MY HEART TO FEAR YOUR
> NAME.
>
> Psalm 86:11

Today's Living Word

Date:

Today's Scripture Passage:

Key Verse

Notes and Observations:
(What does this say? What catches my attention? What do I not understand—or want to know more about?)

Going Deeper:
(How does this touch my life? What is God saying to me?)

_____

_____

_____

_____

_____

_____

My Prayer Response:
(How will I live this Word today?)

_____

_____

_____

_____

_____

> IF ANY OF YOU LACKS WISDOM, LET HIM ASK GOD, WHO GIVES TO ALL ... GENEROUSLY AND WITHOUT REPROACHING.
>
> James 1:5

Today's Living Word

Date: _____

Today's Scripture Passage: _____

Key Verse

Notes and Observations:
(What does this say? What catches my attention? What do I not understand—or want to know more about?)

Going Deeper:

(How does this touch my life? What is God saying to me?)

_____

_____

_____

_____

_____

_____

My Prayer Response:

(How will I live this Word today?)

_____

_____

_____

_____

_____

_____

> MY GRACE IS SUFFICIENT FOR YOU, FOR MY POWER IS MADE PERFECT IN WEAKNESS.
>
> 2 Corinthians 12:9

EXAMINE YOURSELVES, TO SEE WHETHER YOU ARE HOLDING TO YOUR FAITH.

2 Corinthians 13:5

In the past ten days of journaling, the scripture that has meant most to me is:

My biggest aha moment was:

I learned this about God:

I am especially thankful for:

Lord, please help me to:

> The more we've learned God's Word by heart, the more we find it showing up in our moments of need. . . .
>
> What situations in your life often leave you feeling alone or adrift? As you read the scriptures this week, ask the Spirit to lead you to a passage that will help anchor you in God during those struggles. Then take the time to memorize that passage.
>
> Meg Hunter-Kilmer,
> "The Value of Memorizing Scripture," pages 833-34

Today's Living Word

Date:

_____

Today's Scripture Passage:

_____

— *Key Verse* —

Notes and Observations:
(What does this say? What catches my attention? What do I not understand—or want to know more about?)

_____

_____

_____

_____

_____

_____

_____

_____

Going Deeper:
(How does this touch my life? What is God saying to me?)

_____

_____

_____

_____

_____

My Prayer Response:
(How will I live this Word today?)

_____

_____

_____

_____

_____

> MAY THE GOD OF HOPE FILL YOU WITH ALL JOY AND PEACE IN BELIEVING, SO THAT BY THE POWER OF THE HOLY SPIRIT YOU MAY ABOUND IN HOPE.
>
> Romans 15:13

Today's Living Word

Date:

Today's Scripture Passage:

Key Verse

Notes and Observations:
(What does this say? What catches my attention? What do I not understand—or want to know more about?)

Going Deeper:
(How does this touch my life? What is God saying to me?)

My Prayer Response:
(How will I live this Word today?)

> COME TO ME, ALL WHO LABOR AND ARE HEAVY LADEN, AND I WILL GIVE YOU REST.
>
> Matthew 11:28

Today's Living Word

Date:

Today's Scripture Passage:

Key Verse

Notes and Observations:
(What does this say? What catches my attention? What do I not understand—or want to know more about?)

Going Deeper:
(How does this touch my life? What is God saying to me?)

_____

_____

_____

_____

_____

_____

My Prayer Response:
(How will I live this Word today?)

_____

_____

_____

_____

_____

_____

_____

> HE BROUGHT ME TO THE BANQUETING HOUSE, AND HIS BANNER OVER ME WAS LOVE.
>
> Song of Songs 2:4

Today's Living Word

Date: _____

Today's Scripture Passage: _____

Key Verse

Notes and Observations:
(What does this say? What catches my attention? What do I not understand—or want to know more about?)

Going Deeper:
(How does this touch my life? What is God saying to me?)

My Prayer Response:
(How will I live this Word today?)

EVERY WORD OF GOD
PROVES TRUE; HE IS A
SHIELD TO THOSE WHO
TAKE REFUGE IN HIM.

Proverbs 30:5

Today's Living Word

Date: _____

Today's Scripture Passage: _____

Key Verse

Notes and Observations:
(What does this say? What catches my attention? What do I not understand—or want to know more about?)

_____
_____
_____
_____
_____
_____
_____

Going Deeper:
(How does this touch my life? What is God saying to me?)

_____
_____
_____
_____
_____
_____

My Prayer Response:
(How will I live this Word today?)

_____
_____
_____
_____
_____

> LIKE NEWBORN INFANTS, LONG FOR THE PURE SPIRITUAL MILK, THAT BY IT YOU MAY GROW UP TO SALVATION.
>
> 1 Peter 2:2

Date:

_____

Today's Scripture Passage:

_____

Key Verse

Notes and Observations:
(What does this say? What catches my attention? What do I not understand—or want to know more about?)

Going Deeper:
(How does this touch my life? What is God saying to me?)

_____

_____

_____

_____

_____

_____

_____

My Prayer Response:
(How will I live this Word today?)

_____

_____

_____

_____

_____

_____

> WHEN I AM AFRAID,
> I PUT MY TRUST
> IN YOU.
>
> Psalm 56:3

Today's Living Word

Date:
_____

Today's Scripture Passage:
_____

Key Verse

Notes and Observations:
(What does this say? What catches my attention? What do I not understand—or want to know more about?)

_____
_____
_____
_____
_____
_____
_____

Going Deeper:
(How does this touch my life? What is God saying to me?)

My Prayer Response:
(How will I live this Word today?)

> YOU ARE GOD OF THE LOWLY, HELPER OF THE OPPRESSED, UPHOLDER OF THE WEAK, . . . SAVIOR OF THOSE WITHOUT HOPE.
>
> Judith 9:11

Today's Living Word

Date:

_____

Today's Scripture Passage:

_____

— Key Verse —

Notes and Observations:
(What does this say? What catches my attention? What do I not understand—or want to know more about?)

Going Deeper:
(How does this touch my life? What is God saying to me?)

My Prayer Response:
(How will I live this Word today?)

> BE PLEASED, O LORD, TO DELIVER ME! O LORD, MAKE HASTE TO HELP ME!
>
> Psalm 40:13

Today's Living Word

Date:

_____

Today's Scripture Passage:

_____

―― *Key Verse* ――

Notes and Observations:
(What does this say? What catches my attention? What do I not understand—or want to know more about?)

Going Deeper:
(How does this touch my life? What is God saying to me?)

_____

_____

_____

_____

_____

My Prayer Response:
(How will I live this Word today?)

_____

_____

_____

_____

_____

_____

> THE WORD OF THE LORD IS UPRIGHT; AND ALL HIS WORK IS DONE IN FAITHFULNESS.
>
> Psalm 33:4

Today's Living Word

Date:

Today's Scripture Passage:

Key Verse

Notes and Observations:
(What does this say? What catches my attention? What do I not understand—or want to know more about?)

Going Deeper:
(How does this touch my life? What is God saying to me?)

My Prayer Response:
(How will I live this Word today?)

> GOD SO LOVED THE WORLD THAT HE GAVE HIS ONLY-BEGOTTEN SON, THAT WHOEVER BELIEVES IN HIM SHOULD NOT PERISH BUT HAVE ETERNAL LIFE.
>
> John 3:16

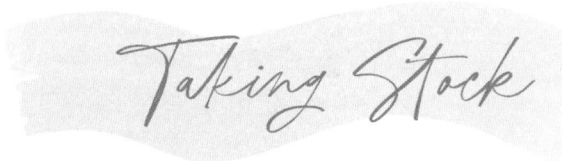

Taking Stock

EXAMINE YOURSELVES, TO SEE WHETHER YOU ARE HOLDING TO YOUR FAITH.

2 Corinthians 13:5

In the past ten days of journaling, the scripture that has meant most to me is:

_____

_____

_____

My biggest aha moment was:

_____

_____

_____

I learned this about God:

_____

_____

I am especially thankful for:

Lord, please help me to:

> At times we might feel like we need to go or grow in our own direction and believe that if only God would answer our prayers the way we desire, we would be doing great things for him and the Church. But God knows us better than we know ourselves, and if we trust in the True Vine, Jesus, we will receive the blessings that come to those who abide.
>
> Teresa Tomeo, "Life in the Vine," page 1647

AND THIS IS THE CONFIDENCE WHICH WE HAVE IN HIM, THAT IF WE ASK ANYTHING ACCORDING TO HIS WILL *he hears us.*

1 John 5:14

My Prayer Intentions

FOR OTHERS

DATE	INTENTION	SCRIPTURE

> PRAY AT ALL TIMES IN THE SPIRIT,
> WITH ALL PRAYER AND SUPPLICATION.
> TO THAT END KEEP ALERT WITH ALL
> PERSEVERANCE, MAKING SUPPLICATION
> FOR ALL THE SAINTS.
>
> Ephesians 6:18

IN GRATITUDE

DATE	THANKSGIVING	SCRIPTURE

> REJOICE ALWAYS, PRAY CONSTANTLY, GIVE THANKS IN ALL CIRCUMSTANCES; FOR THIS IS THE WILL OF GOD IN CHRIST JESUS FOR YOU.
>
> 1 Thessalonians 5:16-18

MY PRAYER INTENTIONS

FOR MYSELF

DATE	INTENTION	SCRIPTURE

HAVE NO ANXIETY ABOUT ANYTHING, BUT IN EVERYTHING BY PRAYER AND SUPPLICATION WITH THANKSGIVING LET YOUR REQUESTS BE MADE KNOWN TO GOD. AND THE PEACE OF GOD, WHICH PASSES ALL UNDERSTANDING, WILL KEEP YOUR HEARTS AND YOUR MINDS IN CHRIST JESUS.

Philippians 4:6-7

WHEN WE READ SCRIPTURE PRAYERFULLY AS MEMBERS OF CHRIST'S BRIDE, THE CHURCH, WE READ AS PART OF A LARGER MYSTICAL AND ECCLESIAL CONVERSATION.

AS WE READ THE SCRIPTURES, AND ENCOUNTER WOMEN SUCH AS SARAH, HANNAH, RUTH, SALOME, AND, ABOVE ALL, MARY, WE "PONDER" SCRIPTURE IN OUR HEARTS WITH THEM. AND WE CAN BE INSPIRED BY THEIR SPIRITUAL FRIENDSHIP TO BECOME LIVING SCRIPTURES OURSELVES (SEE DV 8). IN OTHER WORDS, WE MAY SO GROW IN OUR DESIRE TO BE FORMED BY OUR CONVERSATION WITH CHRIST THAT WE JUST MIGHT BE MOVED BY OUR LOVE FOR HIM TO DO AS HE ASKS: "LOVE ONE ANOTHER AS I HAVE LOVED YOU."

Catherine Cavadini, "Illuminating Fire," page xviii

Women of the Word Index

Discover how the lives of these biblical "Women of the Word" have inspired contemporary women as you read the stories along with their portraits in the *Living the Word Catholic Women's Bible*.

Abigail, portrait, 391; 1 Sam 25
Anna the prophetess, portrait, 1571; Lk 2:36–38
Athaliah, portrait, 571; 2 Kings 8:26, 11; 2 Chron 22; 23:13–21; 24:7
Bathsheba, portrait, 435; 2 Sam 11:2, 3; 12:24; 1 Kings 1:11–31; 2:13–19; 1 Chron 3:5
"Bent over" woman, portrait, 1597; Lk 13:10–17
Bleeding woman, portrait, 1536; Mt 9:20–22; Mk 5:25–34; Lk 8:43–48
Deborah, portrait, 319; Judg 4–5
Dinah, portrait, 59; Gen 34
Elizabeth, portrait, 1568; Lk 1:5–80
Eunice, portrait, 1827; 2 Tim 1:5
Eve, portrait, 12; Gen 2–3
God's "unfaithful bride," portrait, 1229; Ezek 16
Hagar, portrait, 28; Gen 16; 21:9–17; 25:12
Hannah, portrait, 361; 1 Sam 1:2, 5–20, 22–28; 2:1–10, 19–21
Jael, portrait, 319; Judg 4:17–22; 5:6, 24–27
Jairus's daughter, portrait, 1536; Mk 5:2–43
Jehosheba, portrait, 571; 2 Kings 11:2
Jephthah's daughter, portrait, 335; Judg 11
Judith, portrait, 644; Jud 1:1–16:25
Leah, portrait, 81; Gen 29; 30; 49:31; Ruth 4:11
Lois, portrait, 1827; 2 Tim 1:5
Lydia, portrait, 1685; Acts 16:14–15
Martha, portrait, 1589, 1641; Lk 10:38–42; Jn 11:1, 5, 19–28, 30, 38–40; 12:2
Mary, mother of Jesus, portrait, 1565; Mt 1:16; 1:18–25; 2:11; 2:13–23; 12:46–50; 13:55; Mk 3:31–35; 6:3; Lk 1:26–38, 39–45, 46–56; 2:4–7, 16–20, 22–24, 33–35, 39–40, 41–52; 8:19–21; Jn 2:1–5, 12; 6:42; 19:25–27; Acts 1:14; Gal 4:4
Mary, sister of Martha, portrait, 1589; Jn 11:1–2; Lk 10:38–42
Mary Magdalene, portrait, 1558; Mt 27:55–56; 27:61; 28:1–11; Mk 15:40–41, 47; 16:1–8; Lk 8:2–3; 24:10; Jn 19:25; 20:1–2, 11–18
Michal, portrait, 405; 1 Sam 14:49; 17:25; 18:20, 25, 27–28; 19:11–14, 17; 25:44; 2 Sam 3:13–16; 6:16, 20–23; 1 Chron 15:29
Miriam, portrait, 207; Ex 2:4, 7–9; 15:20–21; Num 12:1, 4–5, 10, 12, 14–15; 20:1; 26:59; Deut 24:9; 1 Chron 6:3; Micah 6:4
Mother of seven sons, portrait, 1451; 2 Mac 7
Naomi, portrait, 351; Ruth 1:1–3, 5–8, 10–22; 2:1–2, 6, 11, 18–20, 22–23; 3:1–6, 16–18; 4:3, 5, 9, 14–17
Phoebe, portrait, 1724; Rom 16:1
Priscilla, portrait, 1746; Acts 18:2, 18–19, 26; Rom 16:3–4; 1 Cor 16:19; 2 Tim 4:19
Puah, portrait, 87; Ex 1:15
Queen of Sheba, portrait, 451; Gen 10; 1 Kings 10:1–13; 2 Chron 9:1–12; Mt 12:42; Lk 11:31
Rachel, portrait, 49; Gen 29:6, 9–13, 16–18, 20–21, 25, 27–30, 31; 30:1–8, 14–15, 22–25; 31:4, 14, 17, 19, 26, 28, 31–35, 41, 43, 50, 55; 32:22; 33:1–2, 5, 7; 35:16–20, 24; 37:10; 43:29; 44:27; 46:19, 22, 25; 48:7; 1 Sam 10:2; Jer 31:15; Mt 2:18
Rahab, portrait, 283; Josh 2:1–24; 6:17, 22–23, 25; Mt 1:5; Heb 11:31; Jas 2:25
Rebekah, portrait, 40; Gen 21:23; 24:15–67; 25:20–26, 28; 26:7–10, 35; 27:5–17, 42–46; 28:2, 5, 7; 29:10, 13; 35:8; Rom 9:10
Ruth, portrait, 355; Ruth 1:1–4:22; Mt 1:5
Salome, wife of Zebedee, portrait, 1509; Mt 20:20–21; 27:55–56; Mk 15:40; 16:1
Sarah, wife of Abraham, portrait, 23; Gen 11:29–31; 12:5, 11–20; 13:1; 16:1–6, 8–9; 17:15–17, 19, 21; 18:6, 9–15; 20:2–7, 11–14, 16, 18; 21:1–3, 6–7, 9–10, 12; 23:1–3, 19; 24:36; 25:10, 12; 49:31; Is 51:2; Rom 4:19; 9:9; Gal 4:22–24, 26, 30–31; Heb 11:11; 1 Pet 3:6
Sarah, wife of Tobias, portrait, 624; Tob 3:7, 10, 17; 6:11–12; 7:8–10, 12, 16; 8:4; 10:10–12; 11:15, 17; 12:12, 14
Shiphrah, portrait, 87; Ex 1:15

Shulammite woman, portrait, 913; Song
Shunammite woman, portrait, 480; 2 Kings 4:8–37, 8:1–6
Susanna, portrait, 1299; Dan 13
Syrophoenician woman, portrait, 1539; Mk 7:26
Tabitha, portrait, 1673; Acts 9:36
Tamar, portrait, 65; Gen 38
Woman at the well, portrait, 1625; Jn 4:1–26
Woman caught in adultery, portrait, 1632; Jn 8:1–11
Woman clothed with the sun, portrait, 1909; Rev 12
Woman of valor, portrait, 889; Prov 31:10–31
Women at the foot of the Cross, portrait, 1523; Mt 27:55–56; Mk 15:40; Lk 23:49; Jn 19:25
Women of Galilee, portrait, 1582; Lk 23:55
Women in Jesus's genealogy, portrait, 1476; Mt 1:1–16

Notes

GET THE
Companion Bible

 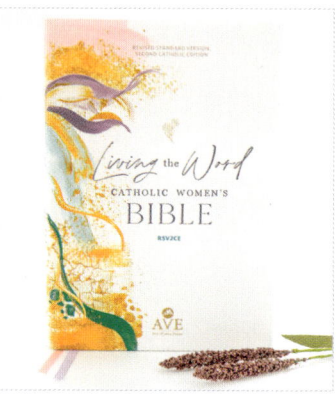 

Do you long to connect with a variety of women just like you who live the Word of God in the world each day?

That connection is what makes the *Living the Word Catholic Women's Bible* different from other Bibles for women: it includes almost four-hundred pages of special features created for women by women—more than forty scholars, teachers, religious, authors, ministers, and speakers—such as Leah Darrow, Sarah Christmyer, Johnnette Benkovic Williams, Meg Hunter-Kilmer, and Sr. Maria Kim-Ngân Bùi, FSP—who come from a variety of backgrounds and reflect the diversity of the Catholic faith. You can walk through scripture in community with other women who seek to become closer to God by reading his Word and living it in their daily lives.

Look for this Bible wherever books and eBooks are sold.
For more information, visit **avemariapress.com/living-the-word**.